Original title:
Eskimo Fashion Show

Copyright © 2024 Creative Arts Management OÜ
All rights reserved.

Author: Riley Donovan
ISBN HARDBACK: 978-9916-94-294-9
ISBN PAPERBACK: 978-9916-94-295-6

Nordic Nights

In boots so big, I trip and fall,
My furry hat, a fashion call.
With mittens bright, I wave hello,
My frozen fingers steal the show.

The parka shines, a brilliant hue,
I strut around like I'm brand new.
With laughs that echo, spirits high,
We dance beneath the starry sky.

Whimsical Wraps

Wrap me up in fluff and fun,
A polar bear could be outdone.
With scarves that twirl and hats that pop,
I'm the jester at the frosty shop.

Chilly cheeks and noses red,
I prance around like a fashion spread.
With laughter ringing, we can't seem,
To stop this wild, winter dream.

Sleet and Sequins

Dazzling sparkles meet the snow,
Sequined boots take center show.
As snowflakes twirl in frosty air,
We giggle as we try to wear.

The crystal flare in every slide,
Turns icy paths to fun-filled rides.
With every slip, we can't resist,
The joy of fashion, a frosty twist.

Fashion on Frozen Lakes

Skating circles, feeling bold,
Breezy styles, a sight to behold.
With polar prints and wavy lines,
Strutting hard across the pines.

Our smiles wide, we giggle loud,
In icy outfits, we feel proud.
With every glide, we laugh and play,
It's a runway vibe in a winter way.

Icy Runway Dreams

When fur meets flair, oh what a sight,
Models tripping in boots too tight.
Snowflakes dance on mismatched hats,
Strutting their stuff, looking like sassy cats.

A parka zipped up to the chin,
Rainbow mittens, oh what a win!
Slipping on ice with grace so rare,
Giggling at styles that go everywhere.

Winter Wardrobe Whispers

Scarves wrapped high, like a cozy twist,
Fashion sense you can't resist.
Layered looks, colors that clash,
Strutting in boots that make quite the splash.

Fluffy pompoms bobbing about,
Is it fashion? There's no doubt!
With every step, a comedic flop,
Ice on the runway, just can't stop!

Polar Chic Parade

Fashion's bold in shades of white,
Capes and colors, oh what a sight!
Gloves that jingle with every wave,
Each outfit daring, none so grave.

With furry hats cocked at a pose,
It's a chilly twist on haute prose.
Slides and glides, laughter fills the air,
Tip-toeing softly, but rocking the flair!

Sledding in Style

On sleds they go, all dressed to thrill,
Outfits that give quite the chill.
Down the hill with a fashionable cheer,
Snowball fights, smiles from ear to ear.

Capes flying high, as they swoosh and slide,
Playing dress-up, with laughter as their guide.
From hot cocoa spills to snowmen galore,
This runway's the snow, forever to explore!

Glimmering Glaciers Gala

Beneath the auroras, they twirl with glee,
Parkas and mittens, a sight to see.
Snowflakes fall like confetti so bright,
Chillin' in style, it's a fashionable night.

With boots that make squishing sounds on the frost,
They strut like penguins, not caring the cost.
Fur hats all askew, they laugh and they prance,
Dancing on ice, giving winter a chance.

Arctic Aura

In layers of color, the crowd finds their flair,
Faux furs and fluff that float in the air.
One slips on ice in a dazzling daze,
A laugh echoes softly, amid the cold haze.

Winter coats jingling, like bells in the breeze,
Outfits of snowflakes, a sight that will please.
With rosy-red cheeks and oversized hats,
They strut and they slide, just like silly cats.

Bundled Beauty

Wrapped up so snug, they're a sight to behold,
In neon bright colors, their stories unfold.
A snowman with swagger, boots made of fluff,
Is this a fashion show? Oh yes, it's enough!

They weave through the snow, like a fashion parade,
With puffy jackets that cannot evade.
Gloves of all patterns and scarves long and wide,
In a world of icy fun, there's nowhere to hide.

Sleigh Ride Styles

On sleighs made of sparkle, they glide with delight,
Waving to the snowmen, a comical sight.
Jingling their bells, they take to the run,
Outfits that gleam like the bright winter sun.

With earmuffs so fluffy, and socks colored loud,
They twirl and they spin, oh look at that crowd!
A parade of laughter, in winter's embrace,
In silly styles, they continue the race.

Furs and Feathers

Furs so fluffy, colors bright,
Penguins strut, what a sight!
Hats of snow, boots of gleam,
Laughs abound in this dream.

Scarves made of icicles hang,
As someone lets out a clang,
Tails twitch with every twirl,
Snowflakes dance in a whirl.

Frigid Fashions

Breezes blow and coats cascade,
Jackets lined with jolly jade.
Bright mittens wave, so amusing,
While ice sculptures keep on snoozing.

Socks that glitter, boots that squeak,
Stylish chaos, so to speak.
A parka here, a tutu there,
Strutting with whimsical flair.

Ice-Cap Creations

Crafted capes from frozen lakes,
Giggles flow as each one shakes.
Designers with their frosty breath,
Challenging warmth in the name of heft.

Stunning shades of winter's kiss,
A spectacle you can't dismiss.
Glittering gowns and beaded frost,
In this frostbite fashion, no cause is lost.

Northern Lights Ensemble

Dressed in hues of green and pink,
Watch as chilly critters wink.
Models posing with frosty flair,
Under twinkling lights in the air.

Funny hats on furry heads,
Laughter echoes where it spreads.
In this show, it's all in fun,
Smile along, 'til the day is done.

Glacial Glamour

In a land of ice and snow,
Fur boots and hats in tow.
With penguins strutting by our side,
Who wore it best? Let's not divide.

Icicles glimmering as we pose,
A fashion show, anything goes!
Scarves wrapped thick, we laugh and shiver,
As snowflakes dance, our spirits deliver.

Glittering parka, bright neon shade,
Who knew such warmth could be made?
Snowball fights in our high heels,
Fashion strangles style, but it appeals!

So grab your mittens, strut along,
In this chilly world, we can't go wrong.
With giggles echoing through the snow,
Glacial glamour steals the show!

Whispers of Winter Wear

Frosty winds and cheeky grins,
Layered outfits, where to begin?
Puffy coats and glimmering feet,
A jingle jangle, quite the feat.

Woolen hats with flaps askew,
One wrong move, they'll fly right through.
Oh look! A faux fur monkey stole,
Thinking big, but oh, so small!

Socks that clash with vibrant tones,
Caught in a whirlwind of icy moans.
But we'll twirl, we'll dance with flair,
Amid the fun of winter wear.

With mitts that match, we strike a pose,
On frozen grass, fashion just flows.
Creamy hot cocoa in hand, so dear,
Whispers of winter bring joy and cheer!

Frostbitten Fabrics

Have you seen the trends up here?
With polar fleece from ear to ear.
Boots that squeak, pants that crack,
Braving winter's chill, we'll never look back.

A crazy patchwork quilted suit,
Moving like a frozen brute.
But with a smile, it's all in fun,
Until it snows, then we all run!

Scarves that tangle, oh what a sight,
Worn like crowns in the pale moonlight.
Tinfoil hats for the snowflake chic,
Fashion on point, or so to speak.

So join the fray, let laughter unfold,
In this winter scene, be bold, be gold.
Frostbitten fabrics, a fashion hit,
Roll with the punches, never quit!

Chic in the Chill

Behold the runway of ice and frost,
As models strut, oh what a cost!
With icy brows and rosy cheeks,
Delivering styles on frigid peaks.

Fluffy boots and sleek leggings tight,
We shimmy and glide in the pale moonlight.
Snowboards act as our fashion props,
Watch us go, we'll never stop!

Trendy earmuffs cover our ears,
While laughter rings, banishing fears.
With a frosty flair, we take a chance,
Chic in the chill, we even dance!

So twirl and pose, don't hold back,
In this winter wonder, let's leave our track.
For in every flurry and flutter we know,
Chic in the chill, we steal the show!

Woolen Wonders

In parkas bright as jellybeans,
They strut their stuff on frozen scenes.
With mittens large and socks that clash,
They twirl about, a woolen splash.

Grandmas knit with love and cheer,
Their styles are bold, let's give a cheer!
With hats like fish, and scarves like snakes,
They're making waves on icy lakes.

Chill Chasers

They dance with snowflakes in a groove,
Wearing boots that make them move.
With earmuffs fluffy like a cloud,
They laugh and spin, they sing aloud.

Socks with stripes and capes that flow,
Look at them go—what a show!
Their balmy breath is like a puff,
Who needs the sun when the style's this tough?

Frostfire Fashion

Running wild in coats so bright,
They shine like stars on winter nights.
With sunglasses on, they flaunt their flair,
A snowball fight—who's got a spare?

Sequined vests and feathered boots,
What a sight, oh what a hoot!
Those furry tails bring one big laugh,
Strutting forth on a frosty path.

Blizzards and Beauty

Twirl and whirl in snowflake gowns,
With giggles ringing all around.
The ice is slick, but watch them glide,
With silly hats, they take it in stride.

Heels that crunch through layers deep,
Making snowmen while they leap.
The frosty air is filled with glee,
In this winter parade, so wild and free!

Chilly Chic

In fur-lined boots, they strut with glee,
Waddling round like a chilly sea.
With mittens bright and parkas bold,
They're breaking the ice, both warm and cold.

Snowflakes twirl around their hats,
As they dance 'neath the winter spats.
With scarves that follow, flowing free,
It's a frosty fashion jubilee!

Cozy Couture Craze

Brrr, behold the layered flair,
Outfits fluffy, beyond compare!
With puffy hoods and beaded threads,
They're rocking styles from snowy beds.

Tassels swinging, all in sync,
Fashion's hottest, don't you think?
In cozy knits and silly tights,
They laugh and twirl in frosty nights.

Snowflake Silhouettes

Round and round in frosty light,
They pose in patterns, oh what a sight!
Glittering in the wintry glow,
Like snowflakes swirling, they steal the show.

With oversized hats and cheeky grins,
The fun begins as each one spins!
Bundled tight like a playful bear,
Their funny strut fills the cold air!

Tundra Textiles

Here comes the cuddly cotton crew,
Funky prints in every hue.
With tails that trail and pom-poms too,
Their playful style is something new.

In tunics bright and leg warmers wide,
They flaunt their look with laugh and pride.
With pockets stuffed full of snow and cheer,
The chill can't stop their wild frontier!

Tundra Tailoring

In the land of snow so bright,
Furry boots are quite the sight.
Pants made of seals, quite a steal,
Up here, fashion has its appeal.

Socks five layers thick, hold tight,
All wrestlers wear them with delight.
Jackets puffy like marshmallows,
Strutting strut with giggly shallows.

Hats with flaps, oh what a tease,
Flapping wide in icy breeze.
With every twirl and twinkling glance,
The tundra turns into a dance.

Ice and Embroidery

Threads of frost weave funny tales,
On bloated parkas, with patchy scales.
Stitching snowflakes, oh so chic,
Frosty fashion's at its peak!

Embroidered seals playing cards,
Laughing loud in stylish yards.
Puffing out with every meal,
A fashionable frozen deal.

Frosted Fashion

Glaciers gleam in models' eyes,
Combining warmth with glitzy fries.
With every step, a crunch resounds,
Puffy coats and polar hounds!

Breezy veils of icy lace,
Snowflakes twirling, set the pace.
Style's so bright, it dims the sun,
In the frosted fun, we run!

Pearls of Permafrost

Diamonds in the snow so flake,
Fur wraps that make the winter quake.
Dressed as fish or maybe seals,
Dripping with style for all appeals.

Pearls twinkling on their sashes,
Strutting high, amid the splashes.
In the tundra, they parade,
Making sure they're not afraid.

Icy Inspirations

In a land where snowflakes dance,
A big coat twirled in a jolly prance.
With boots so fluffy, they'd steal the scene,
A scarf that's a penguin in a fashion dream.

Fur-lined hats that wiggle and sway,
Like furry creatures having a play.
Bright colors flashing, from red to lime,
It's a chilly catwalk, an icy rhyme.

Dressed in Drifts

Beneath the auroras, a sight divine,
With puffy jackets and goggles that shine.
They strut like kings, and queens, oh so bold,
Decked in layers, both warm and gold.

Socks of sealskin, all mismatched flair,
With mittens on feet, what a peculiar pair!
As they slide and glide, the snowflakes scatter,
Each outfit's a laugh, who cares if they chatter?

Furs and Feathers of the Far North

In the frosty arena, a parka parade,
With colorful furs, stylists have played.
Fluffy tailcoats and wild hats align,
Snowflakes applaud; it's a funny design.

They swoosh in their gear, with giggles galore,
One slipped on ice, then rolled on the floor.
A plume of feathers took off with a spin,
Who knew warm fashion could make you grin?

Wintry Wardrobe Wonders

With mittens so big, one can barely wave,
They strut about like they're fashion brave.
Pants made of snow, a marvelous sight,
Each step is a tumble; what a delight!

Chunky boots clomp, in a comical way,
As playful snowflakes come out to play.
In otter coats swirling, they bust out a joke,
Winter's runway, where laughter awoke!

Warm Hearts, Cold Hands

In fluffy boots, they waddle and sway,
With mittens bright, it's a fashion ballet.
Hats like penguins, so snug and round,
They trip on snow, oh, what a sound!

Scarves wrapped tight to keep chills at bay,
Their laughter erupts like a snowball play.
Fuzzy earmuffs dance on their heads,
As they strut the ice like glamorous sleds.

Strutting in the Snow

Feet in the air, with a slip and a slide,
They strike a pose, full of winter pride.
Snowflakes drift on their colorful hats,
As one topples over, oh what a spat!

On frosty runways, they twirl and glide,
With fashionable furs, they take it in stride.
Fashion shows in parks, don't you know?
Twirling 'round trees, oh what a show!

Aurora Borealis Beauties

Shimmering colors dance in the night,
Their outfits lit up, oh what a sight!
With glow-in-the-dark at the tips of their toes,
They stroll through the winter, striking some poses.

Glittering icicles hang from their hats,
Frosty sparkles, like fancy spats.
They giggle and twirl, beneath the night sky,
With a dash of grace, they really fly!

Winter Whimsy

Puffin pants and jackets so grand,
They wander the snow, so quirky and tanned.
Sweaters boasting games of snowball fight,
Chasing each other, in pure delight.

With rubber chickens tucked under each arm,
Waddling along, spreading their charm.
In winter's embrace, they shine and glow,
Making memories in the frosty show.

Snowflakes and Style

In a land where icebergs gleam,
Fashion reigns as a frosty dream.
Fluffy boots and mittens bright,
Strutting past in a snowy light.

With parka styles that sway and spin,
Everyone's trying to outdo their kin.
Scarves wrapped high to shield from freeze,
Yet still they laugh with such great ease.

Colorful hats that dance with flair,
Blowing kisses to the chilly air.
Socks that clash with every stride,
Snowflakes twirl as they take pride.

On the runway of crisp, cold nights,
Each outfit shines with dazzling lights.
With giggles loud and spirits bold,
Winter's show is a sight to behold!

Clad in Cold

Bundled up like a marshmallow,
Cameras flash at every shallow.
Puffy jackets, a sight to see,
Each one screaming, 'Look at me!'

Hats that wiggle like a wave,
Oh, how the crowd's laughter behaves.
Boots that squeak with every step,
In this frosty dance, no time for prep.

Faux fur coats that swish and sway,
Making snowmen envy their display.
Gloves with sequins oh-so-bright,
All shine like stars in the winter night.

Whimsical prints on knitted gear,
A fashion parade, far from severe.
With chuckles and slips on icy ground,
In chilly fashion, we're all renowned!

Modish in the Monolith

In the shadow of a giant ice,
Fashionistas roll the dice.
Sled-runway, icy and real,
Dash through snow with trendy zeal.

Luminescent, outfits gleam,
Reflecting every wintry dream.
Earmuffs larger than the head,
Leave the yard, don't stay in bed.

Stripes and polka dots collide,
Worn by those who take great pride.
Chilly cheeks, but oh so fab,
Every pose is a stylish grab.

So strut your stuff, don't fear the cold,
Show the world how you're bold.
Laughing as we spin and slide,
In the monolith, we take great pride!

Chillingly Beautiful

From icy cliffs, the models pose,
Dressed to impress from head to toes.
Glittering helmets, who wouldn't stare?
Every outfit a frosty affair.

With faux-fur tails and snowflake crowns,
Laughter echoes through snowy towns.
Socks mismatched, yet all in sync,
In this chill, we all take a wink.

Chilly weather, but spirits high,
Everyone's a star under the sky.
With every twirl, they laugh and slide,
Fashion and fun, we wear with pride.

So join this frosty, zany dance,
In the cold, come take a chance.
With gear so bold and smiles so bright,
Chillingly beautiful, a pure delight!

Flurries of Fabrics

In the land where snowflakes flutter,
Fur boots jingle, they don't even mutter.
Scarves twisted in a colorful spin,
An ice-cream cone hat, let fashion win!

Snowman struts in a puffy coat,
What did he wear? A sled for a boat!
Earmuffs blaring, colors so bright,
Chasing winter blues, oh what a sight!

Lollipops made of frost and cheer,
Bring on the snow and winter gear!
With each twirl, a snowdrift's delight,
Let's laugh and dance through the frosty night!

Socks that jingle, hats that glow,
Fashion's a party, don't you know?
So grab your parka, let's hit the street,
With laughter and style, can't be beat!

Stylish Shivers

Chilly winds bring a playful spree,
Woolly sweaters dance with glee.
Turtlenecks whisper, "Look at me!"
While mittens boast of their artistry!

Ice skaters spin in trendy shoes,
With fashion flair, they can't lose.
Glittering caps in a polar breeze,
Fluffy llama coats, oh what a tease!

Beaded snowflakes twinkle and sway,
Matching trousers on a winter's day.
Giggles abound as they take a prance,
In this winter wonder, let's take a chance!

So grab your pals, make a scene,
With frosty air, let's feel the sheen.
Whether chic or silly, have no fear,
In stylish shivers, winter's here!

Icebound Inspirations

A snowflake scarf wrapped up tight,
Sleds glide by, what a sight!
Chunky sweaters, colors galore,
Fashion crinkles knock on my door!

Dancing hats with fuzzy bobbles,
Waddle on ice, hop like squabbles.
With penguin prints in a fray,
The outfits steal winter's gray!

Socks that clash, boots that shine,
Groovy mitts in a wild design.
All around, the laughter grows,
As winter comes, watch how it glows!

Icicles sway in a frozen beat,
Wearing styles, oh so sweet.
With every twirl in this frosty place,
Icebound flair, let's embrace!

Frostbite Finery

With frozen toes and noses red,
Fashionistas strut, they're well-fed.
Layers stacked like a sweet delight,
Fashion's a feast in the icy light!

Snowflakes land on a fancy hat,
A knitted cap that's looking "phat."
Riding sleds in dazzling threads,
Braving winter with stylish spreads!

Laughter bubbles, like hot cocoa,
Sliding down hills, oh look at that show!
Mix and match in autumn's freeze,
Every outfit, sure to please!

So grab your friends and make a scene,
With frosty flair, a vibrant sheen.
In frostbite finery, dance and twirl,
Winter's here, let's give it a whirl!

Whispers of Winter Wear

In fur boots made of fluff,
And goggles that shine bright,
They strut on snowy paths,
Proud to take flight.

Socks that clash oh so loud,
With hats that are too big,
They twirl and they dance,
Like a penguin at a jig.

Mittens that are mismatched,
But stylish beyond compare,
With coats that bubble and bounce,
Laughing without a care.

So grab your furry hat,
And shimmy down the lane,
For winter's got its chic,
And joy that's hard to feign.

Lush Layers of the North

A parka with polka dots,
And earmuffs dipped in cream,
Fashion statements are plenty,
In the land of the icebeam.

Scarves wound round like snakes,
In shades of bubblegum,
They prance through frosty blue,
While eating frozen rum.

Ponchos swirling with flair,
Gleaming like frosty stars,
Winding round and about,
Leaving trails like cars.

So layer up the fun,
With colors bold and bright,
For the snow may be chilly,
But our hearts feel just right.

Boundless Beauty in the Blizzards

Snowflakes kiss the runway,
As laughter fills the air,
In snowsuits with puffy hoods,
They waddle without a care.

Bling on the winter coats,
And shine from neck to toe,
With earmuffs like giant spoons,
They're the talk of the snow.

Sassy boots and mismatched mitts,
Each outfit's quite a sight,
Strutting through the blizzards,
With twinkles in their flight.

So come and join the parade,
Join in the wacky show,
Where winter wear is wild,
And the cold winds love to blow.

Arctic Couture Chronicles

In the land where seals can laugh,
And polar bears can sing,
Fashion flaunts its frosty flair,
With quirky, crazy bling.

Goggles stuck on foreheads,
With scarves that twist like snakes,
They prance along the icebergs,
Making winter fashion fakes.

Puffy pants in pastel hues,
Riding high on everyone,
With boots all mismatched colors,
They bring the icy fun.

So gather near the glaciers,
And let the laughter roll,
For winter's just a canvas,
To paint a jolly soul.

Fashion from the Frost

In a land where snowflakes prance,
Furry boots make penguins dance.
Woolly hats all decked in style,
Mittens waved, they strut a mile.

Chunky scarves that tickle the nose,
Fashion faux pas? No one knows!
With parka fluff and colors bright,
They sashay like stars in the winter night.

Snowballs fly as models glide,
Laughing as they take each stride.
Bunnies eye the runway near,
Hoping for a cozy cheer!

So grab your warmest gear and join,
The frosty fun, let's not disappoint.
In this chilly catwalk spree,
Fashion rule? Warmth is key!

Threads of the North Wind

From the tundra, a catwalk grows,
Where fur-lined coats are all the pros.
With colors bright like auroras gleam,
Waddling models in a winter dream.

Hats like mountains, puffs on top,
With every step, they hop and stop.
Bunny tails and snowy beads,
If warmth is chic, they've got the leads.

Laughter echoes through the cold,
As flapping parkas break the mold.
Chasing snowflakes in a dash,
Watch them twirl, oh what a splash!

They're strutting soft and feeling grand,
In every twirl, they make a stand.
Winter's jest, a frozen scene,
With threads of joy, they're our routine!

Aesthetic of the Arctic

In the chilly breeze, they sway so bold,
Wearing laughter, never cold.
Parkas bright, like candy wraps,
With each twirl, the igloos clap!

Frosty feathers in a jolly mix,
Snowflakes dance, doing their tricks.
Gloves that shine like stars at night,
Each outfit's a frosty delight.

Comets darting in a flurry,
They become snowballs, oh what a hurry!
Facing the cold with giggly grace,
Strut your stuff in this winter place!

With belly laughs, we take a turn,
In the frozen fun, we truly learn.
Dress for the weather, twist and shout,
In the Arctic, we're all about!

Beacon of the Borealis

A light show in fur and fluff,
Where polar bears strut, but not too rough.
Jackets hug like a warm embrace,
Fashion's best in a snowy race!

Hats that wobble, socks that shine,
As snowmen pose, feeling divine.
With every kick, a laugh will ring,
In this winter wonder, hearts take wing.

Spirits bright in a chilly bloom,
Models prance, dispelling gloom.
With every spin, the laughter grows,
Under the lights, their cozy glow!

Strut your style in the frosty scene,
With joy in the air, it's evergreen.
As the night sparkles with delight,
Fashion from frost is truly bright!

Polar Patterns

In furs so bright, they strut and sway,
With boots that honk and hats that play.
Polar bears take notes, they can't compete,
In this icy scene, they chop their feet.

With earmuffs thick, just like a bear,
They flaunt their threads, without a care.
A whirling dance, they shake their fluff,
Who knew the cold could look this tough?

Snowdrift Styles

Mittens loud, in colors bold,
They're strutting snow on icy gold.
With sleds like catwalks gifted flair,
The icy winds become their air.

Hats so big, they cover eyes,
They twirl and leap, like snowflakes fly.
In winter's grasp, they boldly pose,
Like frozen models, striking a rose.

Chic in the Chill

Fuzzy boots and shades so cool,
They prance around, breaking the rule.
With glimmering frost in every seam,
They're living life like a frozen dream.

Scarves so long, they nearly trip,
Every step a wobbly flip.
With laughter loud and giggles bright,
They melt the ice with sheer delight.

Arctic Adornments

Jacket bling that sparkles like snow,
They swagger on, putting on a show.
With fur-lined coats and flashy ties,
Even the penguins stop to rise.

In temperatures that freeze your breath,
They steal the stage, defying death.
With quips and jests, they frolic free,
In a world quite warm with their comedy.

Radiant in a Blizzard

In fur-lined boots and hats so grand,
They strut and dance on frozen land.
With scarves so bright, they twist and twirl,
While sipping cocoa — what a whirl!

The parka lengths are quite absurd,
Some are chic, while others blurred.
They trip on ice but keep their grace,
Laughing loudly, winning the race.

Their cheeks are rosy, noses red,
Who needs a catwalk? Just follow the sled!
With snowflakes glinting in their hair,
They bring the warmth; it's debonair.

In mittens and pigtails, such a hoot,
The latest trend is a snowman suit!
With jokes and giggles all the way,
Who knew fashion could be this play?

Eskimo Elegance

Dashing through drifts wearing chic furs,
Strutting like models, they cause some blurs.
With oversized hats that cover their eyes,
They twirl and giggle, beneath icy skies.

Their outfits are layered, it's quite the sight,
A rainbow of colors, oh what delight!
But watch your step on that wobbly path,
A slip on the ice? Now that is some wrath!

They sashay and sway with each chilly breeze,
The audience roars, no one can freeze!
With cocoa in hand and laughter so bright,
These stylish snowflakes own the night.

In fur boots and mitts, they are top of the class,
With snowmen clapping, they sure have some sass!
Dripping with charm, winter's pure glee,
Fashion so funny, just wait and see!

Warmth Wrapped in Style

Fuzzy hoods and hats piled high,
As the cold winds whip and fly.
They spin like tops and giggle loud,
Fashionistas in a snowy crowd.

Fluffy skirts trimmed with icy lace,
Each outfit turns winter to a fun race.
With every slip, there's joyful cheer,
Who knew warm wear could bring such year?

They twirl in boots, all colors bright,
While penguins applaud — what a sight!
In mittens that jingle, they glide and stomp,
With each little dance, they leap and romp.

The warmth they wear is joy revealed,
On frozen runways, they truly wield.
With laughter sprouting like winter's bloom,
Forget the chill; it's a style that'll zoom!

Glacial Gowns

In gowns of white that shimmer and shine,
Silvery threads, oh how they intertwine!
They slide on ice like graceful swans,
With each twirl, the crowd responds.

Their hats like clouds, with feathers spry,
Laughing loudly as they slip by.
With icicles dangling from every seam,
These glacial gowns birth a winter dream.

They waddle like penguins, what a show!
Through snowdrifts deep, they glide and glow.
With mugs of cocoa held overhead,
Who knew winter could fill us with dread?

With funny antics, they trip and cheer,
On this icy runway, there's nothing to fear.
Wrapped up snug, in style so grand,
They bring the heat with a frosty hand!

Glacial Elegance

In furs so thick, they waddle with glee,
Fashionista seals, dancing wild and free.
Ice blocks for shoes, oh what a sight!
Strutting on glaciers, dazzling the night.

With snowflake hats, they twirl and swirl,
Bears in the audience give a low growl.
Outfits so bright, they dazzle the cold,
Frosty fun fashion, a sight to behold.

Threads of the North

Knitted from warmth, with colors so bold,
Rabbits in scarves, their stories unfold.
Worn by the brave, the clumsy, the grand,
Fashion from fur, in a chilly wonderland.

Bubbles of laughter, they tumble and twist,
Wrapped up so snug, it's hard to resist.
With mittens like clouds and hats shaped like fish,
It's truly a sight—now, that's quite the dish!

Snowbound Styling

Boots made of ice, they stomp with delight,
Snowflakes are diamonds, sparkling bright.
With puffs and poofs, they strut down the lane,
Looking for mischief, and causing a rain.

Panda on the runway, what a strange show,
In winter's embrace, they put on a glow.
From toques to earmuffs, in styles that amuse,
Each step's a giggle, in playful hues.

Aurora Attire

Colors of light, in a dance overhead,
Models in layers, all snug in their bed.
With twinkling wishes, and socks made of fluff,
They showcase their outfits, the warm and the tough.

As northern lights shimmer, they shimmy and shake,
In whimsical styles, they're snowflake-bake.
Boys in sleds, and girls with great flair,
Fashion so funny, it's beyond compare!

Frigid Fabrics

In polar fleeces, we strut and sway,
Dressed like snowmen on a runway display.
With hats so fluffy, they float in the breeze,
Watch out! Here comes a flurry of freeze!

Boots like tanks, they stomp and crunch,
We've turned the chill into a fashionable punch.
Scarves so long, they could double as ropes,
Twirling in winter, we're full of hopes!

Gloves with fingers, just a tad too tight,
For catching snowballs, we must hold them right.
On this frosty stage, with laughter in tow,
We'll shimmy and shake in our chilly show!

So come join the fun, in layers we glow,
From polka dots to plaid, it's quite the tableau!
With fashion that warms, we take to the ice,
Making chilly garments look oh-so-nice!

Glacial Runway

Sealskin parkas with pockets galore,
Walking like penguins, we can't take it more.
Beads made of ice, they jingle and chime,
On our glacial runway, we frolic in rhyme!

Tails of our coats, trailing behind,
While everyone wonders, "What is their kind?"
Our mittens so mismatched, a vibrant delight,
Laughing so hard, we nearly take flight!

Waddle and giggle, as we twirl and glide,
Fashion's a frolic, it's a slippery ride.
With each icy step, we own the scene,
A laughable sight, in our frost-covered sheen!

So grab your furs, and swirl around fast,
This glacial bash is a win for the cast.
In colors so bright, like a sun on the snow,
We'll dazzle the crowds with our icy tableau!

Arctic Couture

In polar prints, we strut with glee,
Our furry coats dance as wild as can be.
Accessorize with snowflakes, frozen and neat,
In this arctic couture, we can't be beat!

With boots that sparkle, and eyes that gleam,
We slide on the ice, like living a dream.
Fashion is fun, and laughter is free,
Watch us twirl in glee, just you wait and see!

Socks pulled up high, in colors so bold,
Our unique style is a sight to behold.
With tiny snowballs as our joyful flair,
We strut down the path without a care!

Snug and cozy in our fluffy spree,
Waddling with pride, just you and me.
Together we dance, under frosty skies,
Creating a runway, where the laughter flies!

Frosted Stitches

Sweaters so bright, they could light up the night,
Each stitch a story, in patterns so bright.
With sequined snowflakes pinned on our chests,
We're here for the giggles and wintertime quests!

Watch as we whirl in our quilted delight,
Creating a frenzy, a marvelous sight.
With hats that are fluffy and scarves in a twist,
Our fashion show is one you can't miss!

Torn and patched, our garments are wild,
Like a closet exploded, oh the joy of the piled!
With chuckles and smiles, we dance through the snow,
This frosted ensemble a whimsical show!

Laughter erupts with each playful pose,
In layers of warmth, we outshine the cold.
With a wink and a giggle, we take our bow,
Making memories here, it's fun—this we vow!

Arctic Artistry

In furs and boots, they strut with flair,
A polar twist in the chilly air.
With mittens bright and scarves that twirl,
They swirl and bounce, oh what a whirl!

Giant parkas decked in glittering ice,
Every outfit's a chilly slice.
They wink and pose with snowflakes in hair,
Fashionistas of the frosty lair!

Beads of frost hang like jewels on coats,
While warming smiles will surely gloat.
A snowball fight? Oh what a show!
Style with laughter, let the fun flow!

With glaciers as the backdrop so bright,
Chasing the cold with sheer delight.
It's a frosty runway, pure charm on display,
Fashion fun in the snow all day!

Sleet and Style

Under gray skies with flurries of sleet,
They sashay and roll like winter's heartbeat.
With colorful boots splashed in the slush,
Strutting their stuff with a preppy hush!

Parka pockets filled with snacks galore,
Hot cocoa spills on the frosty floor.
Socks with stripes and mismatched flair,
Who cares when you're chic in polar wear!

Snowflakes falling like confetti in grace,
They twirl and giggle in this brisk race.
A runway of ice where the snowmen cheer,
Sleet and style, a fashion frontier!

With laughter echoing through the cold night,
They prance and play, a comical sight.
Creating warmth where chill might prevail,
In the realm of fun, they shall not fail!

Haute Wear in the Harsh

Dressed in layers that puff and float,
Muffin hats on heads, they happily gloat.
Walk like penguins, waddle and sway,
Haute designs that steal the day!

Socks over snow boots, what a trend,
With a playful grin, the cold they fend.
Laughter escapes as they trip and fall,
Yet in their heart, they stand so tall!

Fleece-lined leggings cause a warm stir,
When winter winds howl, they just prefer
The cozy touch of style on a freeze,
Dancing with joy on a snow-white tease!

Snowflakes cling to their fanciful hoods,
Fashion queens in misunderstood woods.
Through harsh winds, their spirits gleam bright,
In the heart of the chill, they ignite the night!

The Winter Weaver's Show

A cascade of colors, a bumpy parade,
Furry boots shuffle in a playful charade.
With hats that wobble and sashes that sway,
The winter weavers put on a display!

Feathers and fur, a mix so absurd,
Each outfit is as loud as a wintery bird.
Giggling models with cheeks rosy red,
Showcasing styles while they leap ahead!

Pom-poms bouncing on top of their hats,
Frolicking as gracefully as hefty cats.
With scarves that twinkle and collars askew,
They shimmy and shake, oh who knew?

From snowy paths to the frosty glade,
A runway of fun is perfectly laid.
Laughter and colors light up the chill,
In this quirky show, there's laughter to spill!

Icebound Adornments

Furry boots and hats that sway,
With every step, they dance and play.
Sparkles in the chilly air,
Who knew fashion could be so rare?

Fluffy jackets, tailored right,
Strutting 'neath the northern light.
Gloves of knitted wool and cheer,
Let's pose, it's our time of year!

Crazy colors, loud and bright,
Who wore it best? We'll have a fight!
Scarves that twirl in frosty breeze,
Warmth and style with perfect ease!

Frosty eyebrows, cheeks that glow,
Fashionistas, ready to show.
With laughter echoing, off we go,
Icebound fun, a dazzling show!

Sleigh Styles

Sleigh bells ringing, we're in gear,
Dressed to thrill, let's give a cheer!
Riding fast, a stylish scene,
Gliding through the snowy sheen.

Dashing jackets, red and blue,
Fur-lined collars all in view.
With every turn, we hoot and shout,
Who needs a runway? We're out and about!

Mittens oversized, a cozy touch,
Bumping into friends, we laugh so much.
The slushy slopes provide a stage,
Unruly styles at every age!

Every twirl, a joyful spin,
Bringing warmth from deep within.
Sleigh styles that make us grin,
In this fun, we're all winners!

Feathered Warmth

Fluffy feathers in a row,
Who wore it best? No one knows!
Tickling noses, puffs of white,
Fashion finds in snowy light.

Wadded jackets, oh so chic,
Underneath, we'll play hide and seek.
Hoods that cradle cheeks so round,
In this wonderland, joy is found!

Waddle like a penguin crew,
Strutting fluffy, that's our cue!
Giggles mix with frosty air,
Feathered warmth beyond compare.

With each outfit, laughter glows,
The runway's where our spirit flows.
Wearing pride beneath the snow,
Fashion's fun, as we all know!

Shimmering Snowscapes

In shimmering hues, we take the stage,
Mismatched patterns set the gauge.
Snowflakes dance in swirling light,
With hats that make us look just right.

Boots that sparkle, strut and sway,
Who needs summer? We're here to play!
Leaping through drifts with glee and zest,
In winter garb, we are the best!

With every step, the laughter grows,
Frosty breath in shiny shows.
Jumpsuits bright, a comical sight,
Oh what fun, it's pure delight!

So join our troupe, let's all unite,
With giggles bright and spirits light.
In shimmering snowscapes, we'll arrange,
A fashion bash that won't change!

Elegant Expeditions

In outfits made from fluffy snow,
They strut with pride, a chilly show.
With boots so big, they stomp and glide,
On icy runways, they take their stride.

In parkas layered, colors clash,
They turn and twist, oh what a splash!
The crowd erupts in joyous laughter,
As someone trips—oh, what a disaster!

Their hats adorned with furry flair,
They pose for selfies, unaware of care.
With mittens waving like crazy fans,
Each twirl enlivens frosty plans.

But warmth is key in this cold land,
Dressed to the nines, they need a hand.
With furs and feathers, it's a wild ride,
In this whimsical world where fashion's applied.

Fur-lined Fantasies

Beneath the aurora, outfits gleam,
They shimmy and shake, it's quite the dream.
In fluffy coats and matching boots,
They dance around like happy brutes.

Faux fur fluffs and sequins spark,
The runway's lit, no fear of dark.
As polar bears strut, they steal the scene,
With tails wagging, they're quite the machine.

A mishap happens—oh, what a sight!
A pair of goggles, fluttering, takes flight.
Their laughter echoes across the snow,
In this frosty land where good vibes flow.

With sparkly gloves and hats askew,
They wave hello like penguins do.
In this chilly circus, full of glee,
Fashion's a thrill, wild and free!

Cascade of Colors

A splash of hues on frozen ground,
With wacky styles, they twirl around.
From neon greens to vibrant blues,
Each outfit shines, they can't lose!

Boots that honk and jackets that rattle,
They prance along, a merry battle.
In swirling patterns and silly prints,
They flaunt their flair, no hint of hints!

With scarves that flow like magic streams,
They giggle and pose, living their dreams.
In peacoats brimming with fun and cheer,
They leap and twirl—see, there's no fear!

A snowball flies, oh what a mess,
They laugh it off, no time to stress.
With cheers and jeers, they parade with glee,
In this color explosion, wild and free!

Cold Empyrean Couture

Under twinkling stars, they strut with flair,
In frosty garb that's beyond compare.
With capes that billow and socks so bright,
They bring the chill, yet feel just right.

Giggles resound as fur hats fly,
All eyes on them, oh me, oh my!
In boots that squeak and mittens that sway,
Fashion takes flight in the cold, hooray!

With every turn, they twirl and spin,
It's hard to tell where the fun begins.
As flurries dance in whimsical ways,
They light up the night with their playful displays.

With feathers tickling and laughter loud,
They own this runway, oh, be so proud!
In this chilly gala, fun leads the race,
As they playfully warm the frosty space.

Arctic Elegance

In furs so thick, they strut about,
With jokes and laughs, no room for doubt.
They twirl and glide on ice so bright,
In winter wear, they steal the sight.

With boots that squeak on frozen ground,
Each clumsy step, a giggle found.
Hats like igloos atop their heads,
A fashion show where fun embeds.

Scarves so long, they trip and fall,
But laughter echoes, that's the call.
They pose and pout, a silly spree,
In jackets warm, oh what a glee!

From fur-lined gloves to snowy caps,
They spin and dance, in playful laps.
In this cold place, joy does ignite,
Who knew warm clothes could feel so light?

Threads of the Frozen Tundra

In colors bright, they walk with flair,
Puffy coats and mismatched hair.
With whiskered smiles and snowsuit style,
A frosty show, they'll make you smile.

The llamas laugh, their fashion sense,
With polka dots so magnificent.
They waddle past in furry boots,
The crowd erupts in joyful hoots.

A parka here, a beanie there,
Dancing to the chilled, fresh air.
They spin in place, their breath so puffy,
In winterwear that's oh so scruffy!

With each silly step, the chill is gone,
In the frozen world, it's a winter con.
They flaunt their styles, it's pure delight,
Their fashion flair shines ever bright!

Snowy Catwalks

On ice they strut, with heavy boots,
Snowflakes fall like glittering flutes.
In furry coats, they laugh and play,
On snowy catwalks, hip hip hooray!

The models spin, too bold to fall,
In twinkling lights, they have a ball.
With fluffy hats, they dance about,
In cozy clothes, no hint of doubt.

With poses grand on frozen lakes,
Giggles explode with every shake.
A tumble here, a playful bump,
Everyone cheers with a joyous thump!

In this chilly show, they've found their groove,
Fashion and fun, they always move.
With every flash of the frosty breeze,
They revel in warmth, for life's a tease!

Northern Lights

Beneath bright skies, they prance and glide,
In colors that pop, filled with pride.
With sequins shimmering like stars,
They twirl like comets, dancing far!

The jackets puffed, like marshmallow treats,
Silly faces, on chilly streets.
They wave to penguins, feeling bold,
In winter's chill, it's laughter gold!

With woolly socks and mismatched scarves,
Each playful step, the crowd itcharves.
A runway made of pure white ice,
In mischievous glee, they roll the dice.

As lights above, they brightly dance,
Each outfit bold, a daring chance.
With joy that's endless, laughter loud,
Their frosty fashion makes them proud!

Wispy Furs

In wispy furs that flutter high,
They strut like peacocks, oh my, oh my!
With twinkling eyes and noses red,
They fashion walk, enough said!

The gloves are mismatched, but who would care?
Socks on hands? Oh, what a rare flair!
With laughter ringing through the snow,
The runway sparkles, putting on a show.

Each model spins like a whirling snowflake,
Sliding and laughing, oh what a break!
A dazzling twirl in icy air,
Where winter's chill meets joyful flair.

So here they come, in style unbound,
On frozen grounds, their giggles resound.
In garments quirky, hearts are warm,
This wintry scene, a playful norm!

Subzero Styles

Snowflakes fall, coats so bright,
Fur hats dancing, what a sight!
Boots that crunch with every stride,
Fashion strutting, winter's pride.

Colors clash in icy breeze,
Scarves wrapped up like towers, please!
Matching mittens, bright and warm,
Who knew cold could be such charm?

Socks that sparkle, sequins shine,
Frozen fingers? That's just fine!
Gloves with flair, a wild array,
Who cares if they melt away?

Ready, set, let's take a twirl,
In our outfits that unfurl!
Laughs abound as we parade,
Winter's catwalk, perfectly played!

Sledding into Style

Down the hill, we zoom and glide,
Outfits flair while we abide!
Sleds like chariots, we reign supreme,
In our gear, we're living the dream!

Puffy jackets, all the rage,
Strutting forth like we're on stage!
Scarves like trails of falling snow,
Winter glam, it's quite the show!

Racing hats with pom-pom tops,
On these slopes, the laughter hops!
Cheeks so red, but hearts so light,
Fashion's fun in frosty flight!

So grab your sled and show your flair,
Style is found in winter air!
With a giggle and a cheer,
Who knew fashion could bring such cheer?

Shivering in Silk

Silk on snow, what a surprise,
Fashion daring, 'neath frosty skies!
Wrists adorned in frosty lace,
With each chill, we find our grace.

Dancing lightly, toes turn blue,
Are we fools? Well, we think not, too!
Layered hearts in satin dreams,
Laughter echoes; winter schemes!

Paired with fur, oh, what a mix,
Strut the runway, take your picks!
Laden down with beads and shine,
It's the cold that draws the line!

Caught in fashion's frosty grasp,
Chasing warmth with every gasp!
In our gloss, we'll slide and sway,
Winter couture? We say hooray!

Patterns of the Polar

Patterns blend—a wild collage,
Plaid and stripes, a bright montage!
Mittens twirl with polka dots,
Matched with boots—oh, what a plot!

Wildly printed on fluffy coats,
Who knew fashion would get our votes?
Feathers, sequins, making noise,
Jumpsuits for the girls and boys!

Catch those eyes with neon flair,
Wacky hats with bold, bright hair!
Giggling while we strike a pose,
Winter works its funny prose!

On this stage of frosty fate,
Style and fun, we celebrate!
With joy and flair, we dance and play,
In this winter, bright as day!

Milton Keynes UK
Ingram Content Group UK Ltd.
UKHW022342171124
451242UK00007B/106